This book belongs to

....

....

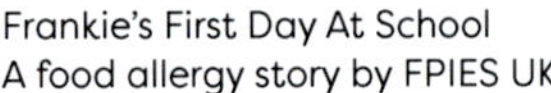

Frankie's First Day At School
A food allergy story by FPIES UK

By Louise Littler

Illustrated by Lisa Williams

ISBN: 978-1-5272-7304-7

First published in 2020

Copyright FPIES UK © 2020
All rights reserved.

FPIES UK is a charitable incorporated organisation registered in England and Wales.
Charity No: 1159635

The rights of the author and illustrator have been asserted in accordance with Sections 77 and 78 of the Copyright Designs and Patents Act, 1988.

No part of this book or its illustrations may be reproduced (including photocopying or storing in any medium by electronic means and whether or not transiently or incidentally to some other use of this publication) without the written permission of the copyright holder except in accordance with the provisions of the Copyright, Design and Patents Act 1988.

Frankie's First Day At School

by Louise Littler

Illustrated by Lisa Williams

It was early in the morning. Frankie **stretched** his arms high in the sky and stepped out of bed with a groannn.

“**Breakfast!**” his mother called from the kitchen. Frankie’s tummy **rumbled** but as he walked into the kitchen his heart sank.

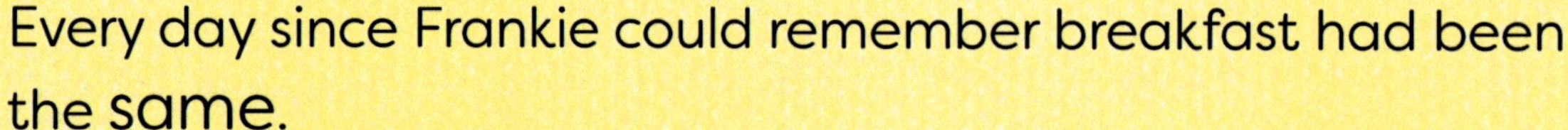

Every day since Frankie could remember breakfast had been the same.

Dinner had been the same.

And as for lunch?

No change there.

There was only ever one thing on the menu ...

Gooberry juice!

Now, it's true that Gooberry juice helps bears grow **big** and **strong**.

The problem was, Gooberry juice was for baby bears.

As Frankie was starting school today he had decided he was most definitely NOT a baby bear anymore.

Frankie **slurped** his juice. Bears are not known for their manners!

He took off his cape and mask and put on his school shirt.

Frankie collected his bag and glanced longingly at his big sister Fern's lunch. A mix of bluefruits, squiggle nuts, hugberries and cheese. Frankie picked up his own lunch box and slowly walked to school with Fern.

Frankie was met at the school gate by a short smiling lady. **"I'm Miss Squirrel, your teacher."**

Fern waved Frankie goodbye. **"I'll see you at assembly. You'll be fine!"**

Hero High

“Welcome to **Hero school,**” said Miss Squirrel. “Here you will learn all the skills needed to become **superheroes** just like your parents.”

The morning went by in a **flash** and Frankie learnt lots about how heroes help people.

A bell rang. "**Lunch time!**" Miss Squirrel announced.

Ahh!
LEAF STRINGS
SQUASH BUDS
SHARK BAR

Frankie opened his lunch box and sighed, "**Ahh.**"
The other children chatted and did not notice Frankie quickly **gulping** down his juice. **Slurrrp!**
(Bears are not known for their manners!)

Frankie however, couldn't help but notice their shark bars, leaf strings, squashbuds and monkey fruits.
He sighed again, "**Ahh.**"

After lunch, the children washed their hands and faces. Another bell sounded.

"Time for assembly!" Miss Squirrel called.

The class lined up and made their way into the school hall. They sat down in neat rows with Frankie's class at the front of the hall.

You can imagine how **surprised** Frankie was to see himself up on the big screen wearing his superhero cape and mask.

He was even more **surprised** to see his sister Fern stand up and make her way to the front of the hall.

"**This is my superhero brother, Frankie,**" she began. The children laughed. After all, Frankie wasn't a superhero yet.

Teehee!
Giggle!

Fern continued, "**My brother Frankie was born a superhero.**"

The children listened carefully.

"**When Frankie was born, we quickly realised he was no ordinary bear cub.**"

"**He has an army of superheroes living in his tummy. These superheroes fight evil forces like germs.**"

The children were impressed.

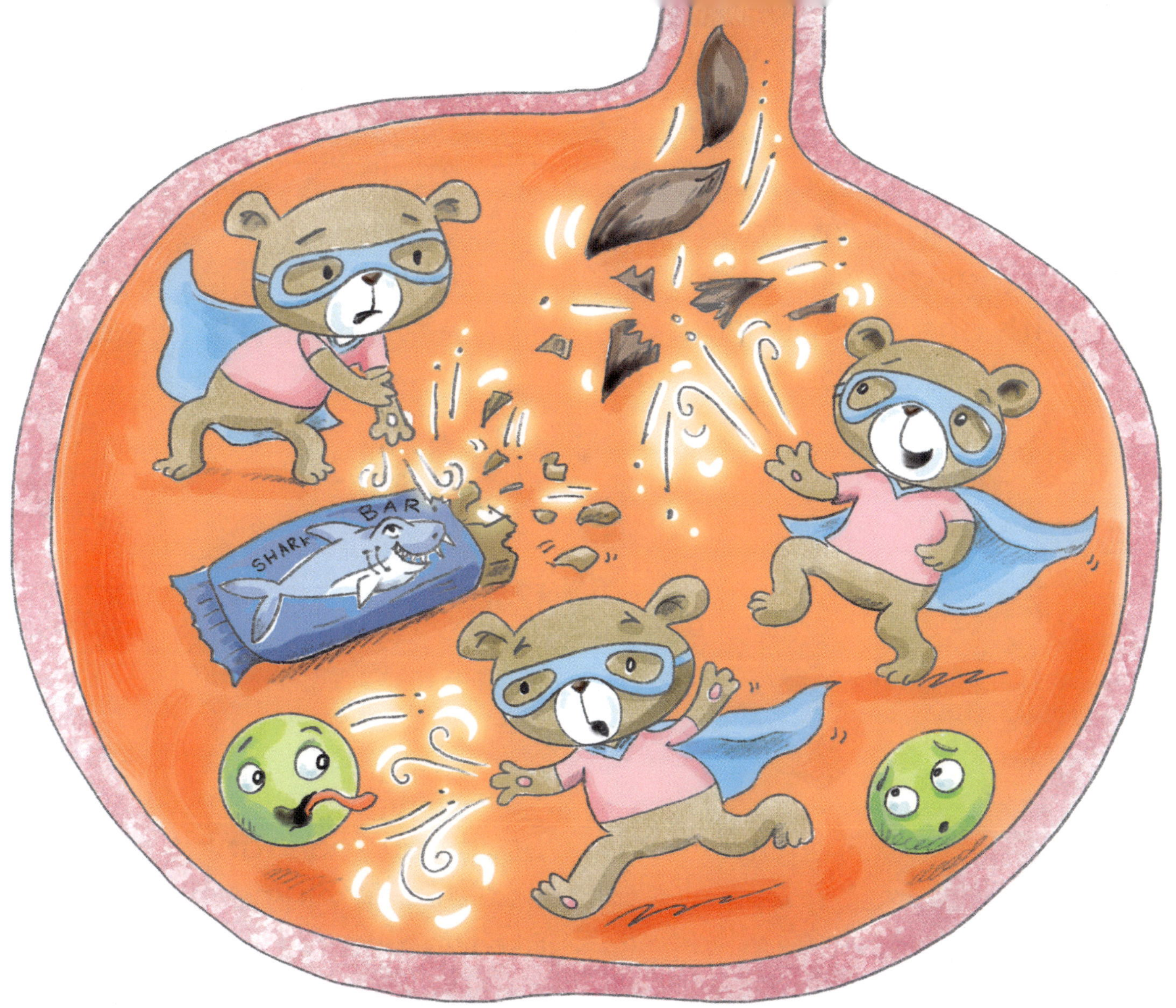

“We all have these tummy superheroes, but Frankie’s superheroes are stronger than yours or mine. His fight everything! Food included.”

“If Frankie eats squashbuds, big fight!
Other foods too.”

"His tummy superheroes try and fight any food he eats," she explained. "With one exception ... They love gooberries!"

"So, if you see Frankie with his Gooberry juice, he's just feeding his tummy superheroes."

"If you see Frankie avoiding your foods, he's just avoiding a tummy fight. This can be quite scary for Frankie."

Fern went on to explain that Frankie had already fought more superhero battles than their parents combined. That he was the **bravest** bear she knew.

Fern turned to Frankie and handed him his cape and mask.

"You've earned these, little brother."

Frankie smiled as he put them on.

At break time he slurped down his Gooberry juice with a smile, picturing it feeding his tummy superheroes. Then he let out a loud **burp!** (Bears, after all, are not known for their manners!)

About the book

Starting school, pre-school or nursery can be an anxious time for parents and carers. This anxiety is magnified in parents and carers of children with food allergies. This book was designed to help parents and teachers to explain food allergies and acceptance to children at this exciting and sometimes scary time. The story follows Frankie on his first day at school as he battles with the feeling of being limited by his restricted diet and how he learns that his differences are in fact a superpower and part of what makes him amazing.

What is FPIES?

* FPIES (pronounced F-pies, like apple pies) stands for Food Protein Induced Enterocolitis Syndrome.
* FPIES is the most severe form of delayed food allergy.
* Babies and children with FPIES become very sick, often become lethargic and may go into shock, one to six hours after eating a problem food.
* Common foods that cause FPIES are milk, soy, rice, oats, chicken, fish and sweet potato.
* But any food can potentially cause a reaction. Even a trace amount of food is enough to make a child with FPIES sick.
* There are no tests available for FPIES, and no way for parents to know which foods may cause these symptoms.
* The only way to know if a food is safe is to feed it to the child and then wait; this is true for every single food an FPIES child tries and can be extremely stressful for parents and carers.

FPIES UK

In September 2013 the Facebook group FPIES UK was founded by the author Louise Littler, after her young son Joseph was diagnosed with the condition. The aim of the group was to provide a safe space for families dealing with the severe food allergy Food Protein Induced Enterocolitis Syndrome within the UK.

In 2014 our trustees, all parents of young children with FPIES, got together and formed the charity FPIES UK.

www.fpiesuk.org

What we do

Our website provides a variety of information & advice for parents & carers and includes a dedicated section for healthcare professionals looking for the latest FPIES management guidance.

The charity also provides a safe space for parents to share their thoughts, feelings and ideas through our FPIES UK Facebook group.

We regularly attend key events and conferences and give talks in order to inform and educate as many doctors, nurses and dietitians as possible.

Our Vision

To see patients with Food Protein Induced Enterocolitis Syndrome accurately diagnosed as early as possible.

For all persons affected by Food Protein Induced Enterocolitis Syndrome to receive the medical and emotional support they need.

Our Mission

To raise awareness of FPIES within the UK.

To provide up to date information to the public, affected families and the medical community.

To provide practical and emotional support to families affected by FPIES.

To provide a sense of belonging and inclusion to children with FPIES.

About the author

Dr Louise Littler is a veterinary surgeon, mum of two and founder of the food allergy charity, FPIES UK. Louise and the Littler family's lives were turned upside down in 2013 when their baby son, Joseph, was diagnosed with IgE mediated food allergies and Food Protein Induced Enterocolitis Syndrome (FPIES).

Having witnessed the lack of understanding and discrimination that children with food allergies experience, Louise was keen to help other children and parents to navigate the challenges by providing a fun and informative resource for parents, carers, and childcare settings. For more information:

www.fpiesuk.org

www.justgiving.com/fpies

enquiries@fpiesuk.org

@FPIESuk

@FPIES_Frankie

About the illustrator

Lisa Williams decided to be an illustrator whilst she was still in primary school. She has been illustrating children's books, magazines and educational material for nearly 25 years. Whilst taking on commercial work, Lisa took a teacher training course, but since qualifying, her commercial success has been such that she hasn't had the time to teach! Lisa is one of the talented illustrators for Team Author UK. This allows her to work with a variety of authors and the opportunity to develop an array of styles.

For more information, visit Lisa's Facebook page:

@lisawilliamsillustration